Patriotic Songs

The Star-Spangled Banner

America's National Anthem and Its History

Written by Francis Scott Key
Edited by Ann Owen • Illustrated by Todd Ouren

Music Adviser: Peter Mercer-Taylor, Ph.D.
Associate Professor of Musicology, University of Minnesota, Minneapolis

Reading Adviser: Susan Kesselring, M.A., Literacy Educator
Rosemount-Apple Valley-Eagan (Minnesota) School District

PiCTURE WiNDOW BOOKS
Minneapolis, Minnesota

Patriotic Songs series editor: Sara E. Hoffmann
Musical arrangement: Elizabeth Temple
Designer: John Moldstad
Page production: Picture Window Books
The illustrations in this book were prepared digitally.

Printed in the United States of America.
1 2 3 4 5 6 08 07 06 05 04 03

Picture Window Books
5115 Excelsior Boulevard
Suite 232
Minneapolis, MN 55416
1-877-845-8392
www.picturewindowbooks.com

Library of Congress Cataloging-in-Publication Data
Key, Francis Scott, 1779-1843.
  The star-spangled banner / by Francis Scott Key ;
edited by Ann Owen ; illustrated by Todd Ouren.
  p. cm. — (Patriotic songs)
Includes index.
Summary: Provides a history and words to three verses of the song called "The Star-Spangled Banner," which became the national anthem of the United States in 1931.
ISBN 1-4048-0175-8
1. Star-spangled banner (Song)—Juvenile literature. 2. National songs—United States—History and criticism—Juvenile literature. [1. Star-spangled banner (Song) 2. National songs—United States. 3. Key, Francis Scott, 1779-1843. 4. United States—History—War of 1812.] I. Owen, Ann, 1953- II. Ouren, Todd, ill. III. Title. IV. Series.
ML3561.S8 K48 2003
782.42'1599'0973—dc21
                                                                    2002155194

O say, can you hear America singing?

America's patriotic songs are a record of the country's history.

Many of these songs were written when the United States was young.

Some songs were inspired by war and some by thoughts of peace and freedom.

They all reflect the country's spirit and dreams.

And the star-spangled banner in triumph shall wave . . .

4

O say, can you see by the dawn's early light

5

what so proudly we hailed
at the twilight's last gleaming;

whose broad stripes and bright stars,
through the perilous fight,

9

o'er the ramparts we watched,
were so gallantly streaming?

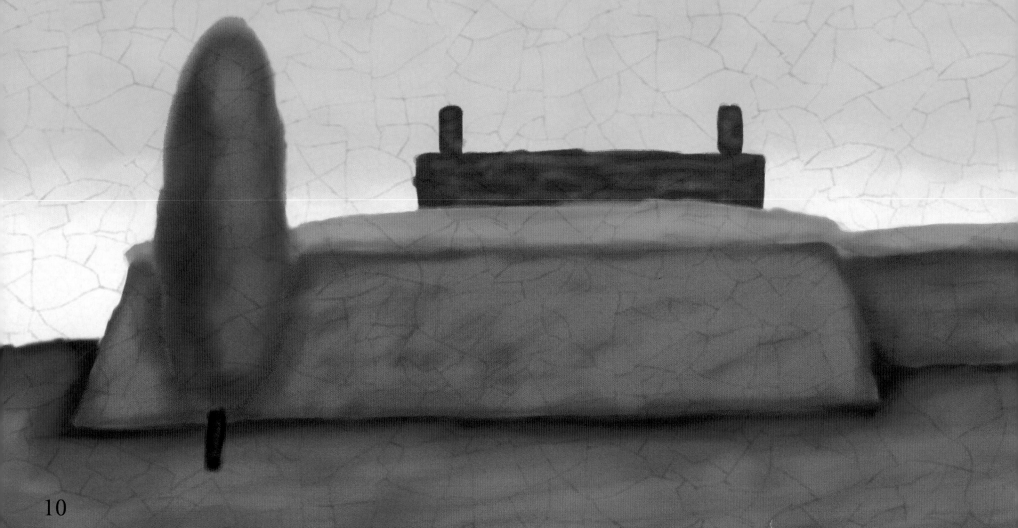

And the rockets' red glare,
the bombs bursting in air,

gave proof through the night
that our flag was still there.

O say, does that star-spangled banner yet wave

o'er the land of the free

19

and the home of the brave?

The Star-Spangled Banner

O__ say, can you see by the dawn's ear-ly light what so proud-ly we

hailed at the twi-light's last glea-ming; whose broad stripes and bright stars, through the

pe-ril-ous fight, o'er the ram-parts we watched, were so gal-lant-ly stream-ing? And the

roc-kets' red glare, the bombs burst-ing in air, gave proof through the night that our

flag was still there. O say, does that__ star-spang-led ban-ner__ yet__

wave__ o'er the land__ of the free and the home of the brave?

On the shore dimly seen through the mists of the deep,
Where the foe's haughty host in dread silence reposes,
What is that which the breeze, o'er the towering steep,
As it fitfully blows, half conceals, half discloses?
Now it catches the gleam of the morning's first beam,
In full glory reflected now shines on the stream,
'Tis the star-spangled banner—O long may it wave
O'er the land of the free and the home of the brave.

O, thus be it ever, when freemen shall stand
Between their loved homes and the war's desolation!
Blest with victory and peace, may the heaven-rescued land
Praise the power that hath made and preserved us a nation.
Then conquer we must, when our cause it is just,
And this be our motto: "In God is our trust,"
And the star-spangled banner in triumph shall wave
O'er the land of the free and the home of the brave!

About the Song

In 1812, the United States went to war with Great Britain. The War of 1812 would last for three years. In August of 1814, British troops captured Washington, D.C. They set fire to the White House, the Capitol, and many other buildings. The British then began to move toward Baltimore, which was guarded by Fort McHenry.

Francis Scott Key lived near Washington. His friend, Dr. William Beanes, had been captured by the British. He was being held on a British ship. President James Madison wrote a letter that gave Francis permission to visit the British commander and ask him to let Dr. Beanes go.

Francis was allowed to board the ship. He soon found out that the British fleet was getting ready to attack Fort McHenry. He had dinner that night with British officers. They agreed to release Dr. Beanes. But the two friends were not allowed to leave the ship until the battle was over.

Early the next morning, the British began bombing Fort McHenry. Francis watched from the deck of the British warship. He knew that as long as he could see the American flag, the fort had not been captured.

The battle continued through the night. Francis watched. When morning came, the flag was still flying. Francis was so excited, he scribbled on an envelope a few lines of poetry that came into his head. He finished the poem the next day and took it to be printed. By the next afternoon the poem, "The Defense of Fort McHenry," was being read all over Baltimore. People began singing it, using the tune of a popular song of the time. "The Defense of Fort McHenry" was soon called "The Star-Spangled Banner." In 1931 it became the national anthem.

Did you know?

The flag that flew over Fort McHenry was so big that each of its 15 stars was about two feet (60 cm) wide. The flag is now in the Smithsonian Institution in Washington, D.C.

You Can Make a Star-Spangled Banner

What you need:

Cardboard

Scissors

Red, white, and blue
construction paper

Aluminum foil

Crayons or markers

String

Tape

What to do:

1. Draw a large star on the cardboard.
2. Cut it out.
3. Use the star to trace other stars on the construction paper and aluminum foil.
4. Cut out the stars.
5. If you like, use the crayons and markers to decorate the stars.
6. Lay out a long piece of string—as long as you want for the banner, plus a little extra for tying.
7. Place your stars along the string, spacing them evenly.
8. Attach the stars by taping the tip of each star to the string. Place the tape over the string so that it sticks to both the front and back of the star.
9. You are ready to hang your star-spangled banner.

To Learn More

At the Library
Binns, Tristan Boyer. *The American Flag.*
Chicago: Heinemann Library, 2001.

Cohn, Amy L. *From Sea to Shining Sea: A Treasury of American Folklore and Folk Songs.* New York: Scholastic, 1993.

Kroll, Steven. *By the Dawn's Early Light: The Story of the Star-Spangled Banner.* New York: Scholastic, 1994.

Ryan, Pam Muñoz. *The Flag We Love.*
Watertown, Mass.: Charlesbridge Pub., 1996.

Yanuck, Debbie L. *The American Flag.*
Mankato, Minn.: Capstone Press, 2003.

On the Web
FirstGov for Kids
http://www.kids.gov
For fun links and information about the United States and its government

National Institute of Environmental Health Sciences Kids' Page: Patriotic Songs
http://www.niehs.nih.gov/kids/musicpatriot.htm
For lyrics and music to your favorite patriotic songs

Want to learn more about patriotic songs?
Visit FACT HOUND at http://www.facthound.com.